JN003121

What Do You Think?

15 Topics for Discussion and Conversation

15のトピックから学ぶ英語ディスカッション

NAN'UN-DO

What Do You Think?

15 Topics for Discussion & Conversation

Copyright© 2023
by
Alan Bossaer

All Rights Reserved.
No part of this book may be reproduced in any form without written permission
from the author and Nan'un-do Co., Ltd.

Download Audio

音声ファイル
無料 DL
のご案内

このテキストの音声を無料で視聴（ストリーミング）・ダウンロードできます。自習用音声としてご活用ください。
以下のサイトにアクセスしてテキスト番号で検索してください。

https://nanun-do.com　テキスト番号［ **512167** ］

※ 無線 LAN（WiFi）に接続してのご利用を推奨いたします。

※ 音声ダウンロードは Zip ファイルでの提供になります。
お使いの機器によっては別途ソフトウェア（アプリケーション）の導入が必要となります。

What Do You Think? 音声ダウンロードページは
左記の QR コードからもご利用になれます。

Read by

Dominic Allen
Emma Howard
Shizuka Anderson

To the Students

Welcome to "**What Do You Think?**", a discussion and conversation book for intermediate-level students. "**What Do You Think?**" is a four-skills textbook (reading/writing/speaking/listening) with a strong focus on speaking and listening through discussion.

Each Unit in the textbook begins with a **Main Discussion Question** where students are asked to give an opinion on the unit's topic. As the students go through the unit, they learn about the process of discussion and how to support their opinions in a clear, logical manner. Often, after working through the unit activities and practice discussions, students are surprised to discover their original opinions have changed. This process of learning more about a topic is part of making an "informed opinion" or "informed decision". What students learn is that often an opinion changes when new ideas are introduced and discussed.

Throughout the 15 units, the students will engage in many pair and group activities which makes learning English more enjoyable, but the pair and group work activities also allow students to hear different ideas and opinions on the various topics. There is also a listening section in each unit where you will hear three different opinions on the topic. The listening section introduces vocabulary but is also a model for a discussion between three people.

Discussion class can be a challenge for students but with practice, all students can become skilled at discussion. I'm sure "**What Do You Think?**" will help you improve your discussion skills and provide plenty of enjoyment.

Table of Contents

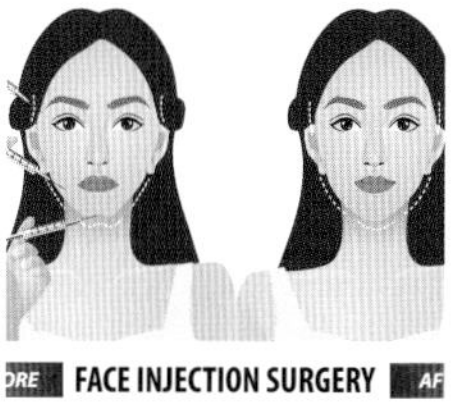
FACE INJECTION SURGERY

Social Network

HOME vs OFFICE

Working at a Convenience Store or a Restaurant?

A Introducing the Topic

Read the passage. Answer the question.

Q: Why are restaurants and convenience stores common places to work for students?

A: They are common places to work for students because there are ____________ ____________ and because many restaurants and convenience stores ____________. Therefore, students have more chances to work after school.

Where Should I Work? 02

Many students these days have part-time jobs. There are many different places where students work part-time but restaurants and convenience stores are common places to work because there are so many of them around the country. In addition, many restaurants and convenience stores remain open late so students have more chances to work after school or in the evening.

Although restaurants and convenience stores are both part of the service industry, working at a restaurant and a convenience store is a different experience. For some students, a convenience store is a better choice. Other students, however, prefer to work at a family restaurant.

Main Discussion Question:

If you had a choice between working at a convenience store or working at a family restaurant, which job would you choose?

I would choose

- a convenience store
- a family restaurant

B Listening – Understanding Various Viewpoints

Listen and choose the answers you hear. More than one answer is possible. 03

1. Chuck would rather work at a convenience store, but it would depend on
   a) the hourly wage b) his co-workers
   c) the working hours d) the location

2. Cassandra would rather work at a family restaurant because
   a) it would be exhausting
   b) she thinks it's an interesting job
   c) working at a convenience store would be boring
   d) she wants free food

3. Ayako would probably work at a convenience store because
   a) serving food at a restaurant seems exhausting
   b) she doesn't like talking to customers
   c) she doesn't think she is strong enough to be a server in a restaurant
   d) she wants an easy job

C Q & A *Write answers to the questions below.*

Q1: What are some of the jobs you have to do at a convenience store?

A1: Well, you have to

a) ______________________________

b) ______________________________

c) ______________________________

d) ______________________________

e) ______________________________

Q2: What are some of the jobs you have to do at a family restaurant?

A2: Well, you have to

a) ______________________________

b) ______________________________

c) ______________________________

d) ______________________________

e) ______________________________

Ask your classmate the two questions. Do you have similar ideas? Add any new ideas.

D Vocabulary

1 *Choose nouns or noun phrases from the list and finish the sentences. If you do not know a word, check your dictionary.*

a) stamina	b) strength	c) patience
d) *good "people" skills		e) a good memory

*good "people" skills = good communication skills or good at talking with people

1. I think if you work as a waiter or waitress, you **need** a, ____________.
2. I think working at a convenience store **requires** ____________.

Go through 1 and 2 (above) with a classmate or in a small group. Give reasons for your answers.

Example: I think if you work as a waiter or waitress, you **need** stamina because waiting tables all day long is tough. You need a lot of ____________.
(Fill in this blank with your own word)

2 *Choose the words from the box to complete the dialogs.*

tough	tired	cash register	strength	dishes
hourly wage	customers	great	a good memory	

Dialog 1

A: Hi Aki. Wow, you look ____________! Are you okay?

B: Oh, hi Tenma. Yeah, I'm okay. I just got off work. I worked an eight-hour shift today at the store. We had so many customers — I worked the ____________ most of the day. We had a sale on cigarettes. You really need ____________. I mean, there are so many brands of cigarettes.

Dialog 2

A: What did you do yesterday?

B: Me? Umm, I had to work at the restaurant.

A: Oh, yeah, that's your new job, right? How's it going?

B: Umm, it's a bit ____________. I mean, it requires a lot of ____________ because the dishes are heavy. But, the ____________ is good so I don't mind it so much. It's good exercise, too.

E Discussion Practice

Discuss these questions with a classmate or in a small group.

Topic: Working at a family restaurant or working at a convenience store

1. Which job is harder — working at a convenience store or a family restaurant?

A: I think working at a ________ is **harder** because ________
________. What do you think?

B: I agree. / I disagree. I think ________.

2. Which job is easier — working at a convenience store or a family restaurant?

A: I think working at a ________ is **easier** because ________
________. What do you think?

B: I agree. / I disagree. I think ________.

3. Which job is more interesting — working at a convenience store or a family restaurant?

A: I think working at a ________ is **more interesting** because ________
________. What do you think?

B: I agree. / I disagree. I think ________.

4. Which job is more boring — working at a convenience store or a family restaurant?

A: I think working at a ________ is **more boring** because ________
________. What do you think?

B: I agree. / I disagree. I think ________.

Change partners and try the dialogs again. Make notes of different responses.

Cash vs Credit Card – Advantages & Disadvantages

A Introducing the Topic

Read the passage. Answer the question.

Q: Why does DeeDee Harris say it might be impossible to stop buying things if she had a credit card?

A: It's because she thinks credit cards ______________________.

Cash or Credit?

04

Are you the kind of person who uses a credit card to buy everything? Or, do you mainly use cash when you buy things? Most people probably use a combination of the two, but some people prefer to use cash as much as possible.

In a recent interview with two women about cash versus credit, Betty Lou Johnson said: "I use cash for everything because I always know how much money I have. If I use a credit card, it's easy to lose track of how much money I'm spending." DeeDee Harris said this: "I've never had a credit card in my life. I mean, I might buy everything I see, if I had a credit card. I mean, credit cards are addictive! It might be impossible to stop buying things."

Main Discussion Question:

If you had a choice between paying for most things with cash or paying for most things with a credit card, which would you choose?

I would choose

- paying with cash.
- paying with a credit card.

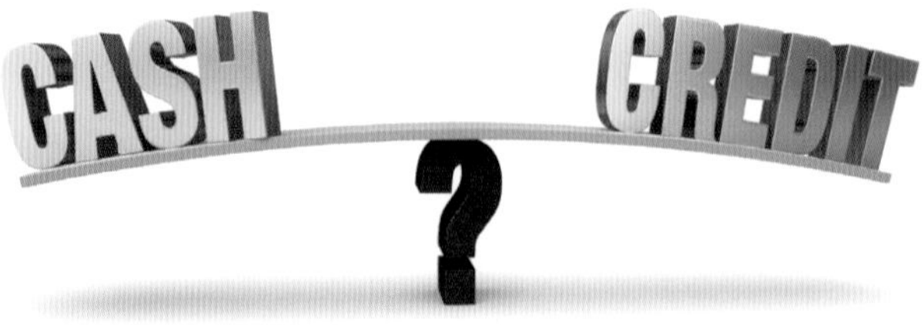

B Listening – Understanding Various Viewpoints

Listen and choose the answers you hear. More than one answer is possible. 05

1. Cassandra thinks having a credit card is
   a) unnecessary b) necessary c) risky d) safe if you are careful

2. Ayako thinks having a credit card is
   a) too convenient
   b) so convenient
   c) not good because people spend too much online
   d) vital

3. Chuck thinks
   a) cash is safer to use
   b) a credit card is safer to use
   c) people should try to pay with cash if possible
   d) sometimes you need a credit card

C Q & A *Ask and answer the questions below with a classmate or in a small group.*

Q1: Do you have a credit card? How long have you had it?

Q2: If you do not have a credit card, do you want one? Is it necessary to have a credit card? Why or why not?

Q3: How often do you use your credit card? Do you think you use it too much?

Q4: What kinds of problems can you have with credit cards? Have any of these problems happened to you?

Q5: Are you strictly a "cash" person? If so, why?
(only)

Q6: If you think having a credit card is vital, at what age would you recommend getting one?

Q7: Do you know any places that require a credit card?

D Vocabulary

1 *Match the words on the left with the BEST meaning on the right.*

This photo matches the word ____________ from the list.

A) inconvenient means ______	1. it's not risky or dangerous
B) vital means ______	2. you need it; it's necessary
C) handy means ______	3. you can't stop using it
D) safe means ______	4. it's useful; it's convenient
E) risky means ______	5. it's not always useful or helpful
F) addictive means ______	6. it's too large and awkward or heavy; it takes up space
G) bulky means ______	7. it could be unsafe or dangerous

2 *With a partner, fill in the blanks in the dialogs. Use the words in the box* ***only once****. There are extra words!*

enough	sums	handy	addictive	bulky	money	difficult	many	easy	case

Dialog 1

A: I want to get a credit card, but I'm not sure if it's a good idea. What do you think?

B: Umm, I think a credit card comes in ______________ sometimes.
(is)

A: Do you think so?

B: Yeah, I mean, sometimes you don't have ______________ cash on you. In that ______________, a credit card is convenient.

Dialog 2

A: Do you have a credit card?

B: Me? Umm, no I don't. Those things are ______________. I mean, some people can't stop using their credit cards. It's too ______________ to buy things with a credit card.

A: Hmm, that's an interesting point. But I don't want to carry large ______________ of cash in my wallet. It could be risky. Also, cash is ______________. It takes up too much space.

E Discussion Practice

With a partner, fill in the blanks in the dialogs. Use words from the box for RED blanks. Use your own language for parts that require an explanation (or example). Your dialogs must make sense. After filling in the dialogs, practice them.

handy	risky	flexible	addictive	vital	inconvenient
bulky	safe	convenient	agree	disagree	overspend

Dialog 1

A: I'd rather use a credit card because carrying lots of cash is ________________.

I mean, ____. (explain)

B: That's a good point, but I think a credit card can also be ________________.

I mean, ____. (explain)

Dialog 2

A: I'd rather use cash because cash is ________________. I mean ____________

____. (explain)

B: That's true, but I think a credit card can also be ________________.

Dialog 3

A: I think you should get a credit card. I mean, a credit card these days is ____________.

B: I completely ________________. I mean, a credit card is ________________

because ____. (explain)

Dialog 4

A: I like using a credit card because it is so ________________. I mean, sometimes cash

is ________________ because you might not have enough **on you** when you want

(on you = with you)

to buy something.

B: I ________________ one hundred percent. A credit card is ________________

sometimes. I think everyone should have at least one credit card.

Doing Volunteer Work

A Introducing the Topic

Read the passage. Answer the question.

Q: What does Haru think about doing volunteer work?

A: She thinks it's ____________________, but it also has some ____________________.

Volunteer Work

06

Parents and teachers often tell children and students that doing volunteer work is important. They might even say that everyone should do volunteer work when they are young. We often see students cleaning garbage on the side of the road and at parks, and sometimes we see a high school or college student coaching young children or assisting elderly people.

Haru Ito, a Japanese college student, remembers being a volunteer basketball coach. "I used to volunteer as a basketball coach for elementary school children. Although I loved coaching basketball and I think doing volunteer work is valuable, it also has some drawbacks. For example, I rarely had free time. I had school, a part-time job, and my volunteer work. I almost never had time to hang out with my friends. Not only that, ..."

Main Discussion Question:

If you have a chance to do volunteer work after you graduate, will you do it?

- Yes, I will try to do volunteer work.
- No, I will not try to do volunteer work.

B Listening – Understanding Various Viewpoints

Listen and choose the answers you hear. More than one answer is possible. 07

1. Cassandra thinks doing volunteer work
   a) is vital
   b) could be tiring in some cases
   c) is not always necessary
   d) makes you a better person

2. Ayako thinks doing volunteer work
   a) can be stressful
   b) can be tiring
   c) is good for your mental health
   d) is valuable

3. Chuck thinks
   a) he would do volunteer work, but it depends on the work
   b) doing volunteer work is honorable
   c) doing volunteer work is everyone's responsibility
   d) doing volunteer work is a good way to meet new people

C Q & A *Ask and answer the questions below with a classmate or in a small group.*

Q1: Do you do volunteer work? What kind of volunteer work do you do?
Have you done any volunteer work? What did you do?

Q2: Do you think it's important to do volunteer work? Why? Why not?
What sort of (= kind of) volunteer work can young people do?

Q3: A volunteer job might be stressful. Why?

Q4: How many hours a week would you do volunteer work?

Q5: Do you think doing volunteer work can be good for your mental health? How?

Q6: Do you think doing volunteer work is valuable?
In what way?

D Vocabulary

1 *Match the words on the left with the BEST meaning on the right.*

A) valuable means ______	1. it's good for your mind/ it refreshes your mind
B) tiring means ______	2. it takes up a lot of your time
C) admirable means ______	3. there are benefits or good things you can get
D) mentally healthy means ______	4. it could cause stress or make you worried
E) time-consuming means ______	5. you feel tired or exhausted
F) stressful means ______	6. people think you are doing a good or nice thing

2 *With a partner, fill in the blanks in the dialogs. Use the words in the box* ***only once****. There are extra words!*

time-consuming	admirable	benefits	challenge
valuable	tiring	tired	resume

Dialog 1

A: What do you think about doing volunteer work?

B: Volunteer work? Umm, I think doing volunteer work is ______________.
I mean, it's a good thing, right? You're doing something good for other people.

A: That's true. But, I think doing volunteer work can sometimes be ______________.
I mean, what if you have school and a part-time job?

B: Good point. You might get pretty ______________. But, I think it's worth it.

Dialog 2

A: I'm thinking about doing some volunteer work. What do you think?

B: Volunteer work? That's a great idea! I think volunteer work is ______________.

A: Really? In what way?

B: Well, it's a good experience and it's also something you can put on your ______________. And, most importantly — you're doing something that ______________ society.

E Discussion Practice

Discuss the Pros and Cons of doing volunteer work. Students A & B will give the pros and students C & D will give the cons. ***OPTION: This dialog can be done with two students instead of four. Write down your ideas (as a team) after your discussion.***

Students A + B - Pros

A: "I think everyone should do volunteer work if they can because ...

A: ____

____.

B: And doing volunteer work is ____________ because ______________

____

____."

Students C + D - Cons

C: "Umm, it's true, doing volunteer work is important, but there are some drawbacks.

C: For one thing, ______________________________________

____.

D: Another drawback is that doing volunteer work ________________

____

____."

Try performing the 4-part dialog in new groups.

Stay-at-home Dads

A Introducing the Topic

Read the passage. Answer the question.

Q: What does breadwinner mean?

A: A breadwinner is the person who ______________________________ to support the family.

What is a Stay-at-home Dad?

08

Have you ever heard the term, "stay-at-home-dad"? A stay-at-home dad is a man who becomes the homemaker in the family. The wife, conversely, is the major breadwinner. The breadwinner is the person who makes the most money to support the family. In other words, the wife works fulltime, while the husband stays at home to look after the children. He also does many of the household chores, and may even do much of the cooking.

In many countries the traditional breadwinner is the man, but some women like the idea of a stay-at-home dad because they have good jobs and they want to have a career. There is also research that shows young children have strong connections with their fathers when the father stays home.

Main Discussion Question: What is your opinion about stay-at-home dads?

Men

- I would be comfortable being a stay-at-home dad.
- I would be uncomfortable being a stay-at-home dad.

Women

- I would be comfortable if my husband or partner was a stay-at-home dad.
- I would be uncomfortable if my husband or partner was a stay-at-home dad.

B Listening – Understanding Various Viewpoints

Listen and choose the answers you hear. More than one answer is possible. 09

1. Ayako
   a) thinks the idea of a stay-at-home dad is modern thinking
   b) thinks the idea of a stay-at-home dad is not common
   c) thinks women are better at taking care of children
   d) thinks men and women can choose what's best for their family

2. Cassandra thinks the idea of a stay-at-home dad
   a) might be stressful for some fathers
   b) is a bit weird
   c) is not accepted in many countries
   d) might be embarrassing for some men and women

3. Chuck thinks
   a) many men are good at taking care of children
   b) women are better at taking care of children
   c) the idea of a stay-at-home dad might be practical (a better idea) because more women have good jobs and good salaries these days.
   d) the traditional way to raise children is not always good

C Q & A *Ask and answer the questions below with a classmate or in a small group.*

Q1: Who is/was the breadwinner in your family?

Q2: Do you think taking care of children is stressful? Why or why not?

Q3: Can men do a good job of taking care of the house? Are they capable?

Q4: Would you be embarrassed to be a stay-at-home dad?
Would you be embarrassed if your husband was a stay-at-home dad?

Q5: Do you think all women are good at taking care of children?

Q6: Are you a modern-thinking person or more traditional? Explain.

D Vocabulary

1 *Match the words on the left with the BEST meaning on the right.*

This photo matches the word ______ from the list.

A) old thinking means ______	1. a situation that causes stress or difficulty
B) capable means ______	2. the old way; the usual way; the traditional way
C) practical means ______	3. you feel uncomfortable (if people know)
D) embarrassing means ______	4. makes sense; a good idea for the situation
E) modern thinking means ______	5. able to do something well; can do something well
F) stressful means ______	6. a new way of thinking; not traditional

2 *With a partner, fill in the blanks in the dialogs. Use the words in the box* ***only once****. There are some extra words that do not fit the dialogs.*

housework	breadwinner	weird	with	salary	modern-thinking
embarrassed	looking after	common	old thinking	capable	practical

Dialog 1

A: What's your opinion about stay-at-home dads?

B: Me? Umm, honestly ... I think it's a bit ______. I mean, it's not really ______ here in Japan. I don't know any stay-at-home dads.

A: I think it's okay. I mean, many men are good at ______ children.

B: Yeah, I agree, some men are great ______ kids, but I think many men wouldn't want to do ______. Umm, that's just my opinion. I mean, I could be wrong.

Dialog 2

A: What's your opinion about stay-at-home dads?

B: Me? Umm, I'm all for it (I completely agree). I mean, men are ______ of taking care of the house and kids.

A: Really? You wouldn't be ______ being a stay-at-home dad?

B: No, not at all. I mean, it's 2023. Women don't have to stay home. And men don't have to be the ______. I mean, my mom's ______ is quite good. And, she loves her job. I think it's more ______ for her to work. My mom and dad share the housework and they both looked after us when we were growing up.

E Discussion Practice

Discuss the Pros and Cons of being a stay-at-home dad. Students A & B will give the pros and students C & D will give the cons. ***OPTION: This dialog can be done with two students instead of four. Write down your ideas (as a team) after your discussion.***

capable	housework	good with	embarrassing	good at
uncomfortable	tough	stressful	feel weird	not common
salary	comfortable	not traditional	old thinking	

Students *A* + B - Pros

A: "I think being a stay-at-home dad is a great idea.

A: ____

____.

B: I also think being a stay-at-home dad is a good idea because ______________

____

____."

Students *C* + D - *Cons*

C: "Umm, I think being a stay-at-home dad has a few benefits, but there are some drawbacks.

C: For one thing, ____

____.

D: Another drawback is that ____

____

____."

Unit 5

Do You Want to be a YouTuber?

A Introducing the Topic

Read the passage. Answer the question.

Q: How many pros (benefits) for being a professional YouTuber are mentioned in the passage?

A: There are ______________ pros for being a professional YouTuber in the passage.

I Want to be a Professional YouTuber!

10

Most people have probably watched videos on YouTube and most people are familiar with the term "YouTuber". In fact, many people who visit YouTube on a regular basis, have one or two favorite YouTubers.
(regularly)

YouTubers are people who create video content on the YouTube platform. Some YouTubers create educational videos, others create funny videos, fan videos, product reviews, and much, much more.

Why would someone want to be a professional YouTuber? Well, for one thing, you can make a lot of money if your site is popular. Secondly, you don't have to work in an office. And of course, you might become famous. Then, you might be able to influence people.

Of course, not everyone wants to be a professional YouTuber. I mean, you have to be talented and creative. And, if you become famous, then your private life will change.

Main Discussion Question:

Would you like to become a professional YouTuber?

- Yes, I would.
- No, I wouldn't.

B Listening – Understanding Various Viewpoints

Listen and choose the answers you hear. More than one answer is possible. 11

1. Cassandra thinks being a professional YouTuber
   a) would be great b) would be tiring c) would be fun d) would be stressful

2. Ayako thinks being a professional YouTuber
   a) would be a good job
   b) would be a tough job
   c) would just be a short-term job
   d) would be a good job because you are the boss

3. Chuck thinks being a professional YouTuber
   a) takes a lot of preparation to make good videos
   b) is only possible for a few people
   c) could be fun because you can be creative
   d) takes a lot of patience because it takes a long time to have a strong following

C Q & A *Ask and answer the questions below with a classmate or in a small group.*

Q1: How often do you watch YouTube videos? Do you think YouTube is addictive? Explain.

Q2: Do you think being a professional YouTuber is a tough job? Why or why not?

Q3: Do you have some favorite YouTubers you follow? Who?

Q4: What kind of YouTube videos are appealing (interesting) to you?

Q5: Do you think being a professional YouTuber is a “real” job? Explain your answer.

Q6: Some YouTubers make a lot of money. How do they make money?

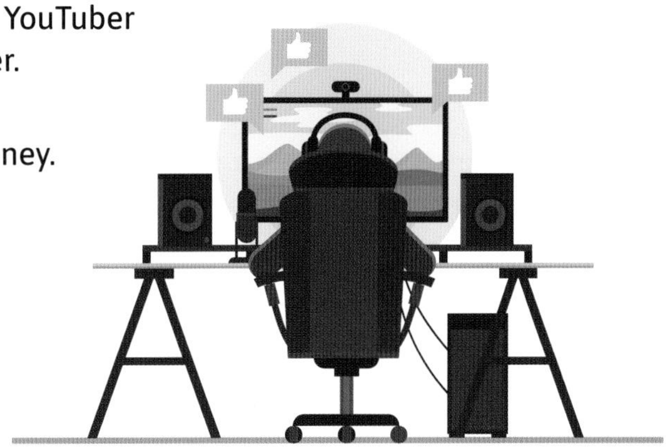

D Vocabulary

1 *Match the words on the left with the BEST meaning on the right.*

A) fun means ______	1. it's enjoyable
B) low-maintenance work means ______	2. you can make a lot of money doing it
C) profitable means ______	3. it's tough or difficult; you feel stress
D) tiring means ______	4. work that is easy to do; not difficult work
E) short-term means ______	5. it could be exhausting: it could make you tired
F) stressful means ______	6. it doesn't last a long time; only for a short time

2 *With a partner, fill in the blanks in the dialogs. Use the words in the box* ***only once****. There are some extra words that do not fit the dialogs.*

profitable	image	creative	imagination	stressful	tiring
low-maintenance	entertaining	boring	short-term	boss	

Dialog 1

A: What's your opinion about being a YouTuber? I mean, would you like to do it **for a living**?

B: Me? Umm, I'm not sure. I mean, I think you have to be quite ______________. Unfortunately, I don't have a good imagination. And, I wonder if you can make enough money.

A: I think if you're good, being a YouTuber can be very ______________. Some YouTubers are quite wealthy.

B: Hmm, but it seems like a ______________ kind of job. I mean, can you do it your whole life? And I think being a YouTuber could be ______________. You're always working.

Dialog 2

A: What's your opinion about YouTubers? I mean, would you like to do it **for a living**?

B: Me? Yeah, I'd love to be a professional YouTuber. I mean, it's a ______________ job. Not much stress at all.

A: Really? I think it could be a ______________ job. I mean, you have to always come up with ideas that people find ______________. So, you're always worrying.

B: Yeah, it could be stressful, but it seems like interesting work. And, you get to be your own ______________.

E Discussion Practice

*With a partner, fill in the blanks in the dialogs. Use words from the box for RED blanks. Use your own language for parts that require an explanation (or example). Your dialogs must make sense. Circle **would be** or **could be** in the dialogs. After filling in the dialogs, practice them.*

could be (use this if you think it's possible but not 100%)

would be (use this if you think it's 100% possible)

fun	tiring	stressful	low-maintenance	profitable
short-term	*lazy	*creative	*hard-working	

*Use these adjectives to describe a person in **Dialog 2**.

Dialog 1

A: I think it would be great to be a professional YouTuber.

B: Really? Do you think so?

\+ A: Yeah. I think it would be/could be ________________. I mean, ________________

____. (explain)

– B: I have to disagree. I think it would be/could be a ________________ job. I mean,

____. (explain)

Dialog 2

A: What do you think about being a professional YouTuber? I mean, do you think it would be a good job?

\+ B: Umm, yeah, I think it could be a good job for someone who is ________________.

And, I think it would be/could be ________________. I mean, ________________

____. (explain)

– A: Yeah, but I think it would be/could be ________________. I mean, ________________

____. (explain)

B: Hmm, ... that's a good point. I guess it depends on the person.

I Want a Driverless Car!

A Introducing the Topic

Read the passage. Answer the question.

Q1: How many pros (benefits) are mentioned in the passage?
There **is/are** ______________ pro(s).

Q2: How many cons (drawbacks) are mentioned in the passage?
There **is/are** ______________ con(s).

I Want a Driverless Car!

12

Can you imagine taking a drive in the countryside without a human driving the car? It sounds like a science fiction movie. But, did you know there are already cars that can operate without a human driver? They are called driverless cars and many car companies are developing them.

Why would anyone want a driverless car? I mean, are there any pros?

The companies that are developing driverless cars think they are safer than cars driven by humans. "A driverless car is really a computer and it can react faster than a human driver", says one car company spokesman. "So, there will be fewer accidents."

Of course, not everyone agrees. One person who loves driving wondered what would happen if the computer crashed while the car was moving. "I think there could be many serious car accidents if the computer crashed". He added, "And, I just think they would be creepy."

Main Discussion Question:
Would you like to have a driverless car?

- Yes, I would.
- No, I wouldn't.

B Listening – Understanding Various Viewpoints

Listen and choose the answers you hear. More than one answer is possible. 13

1. Cassandra thinks owning a driverless car
   a) would be great b) would be boring
   c) would be fun d) would be dangerous

2. Ayako thinks having a driverless car
   a) would be safe b) could be a bit boring
   c) would be economical d) is dangerous because the car might speed

3. Chuck thinks owning a driverless car
   a) would be creepy b) is the way of the future
   c) could be hazardous d) would be comfortable

C Q & A *Ask and answer the questions below with a partner or in a small group.*

Q1: Do you have a driver's license? If you don't, do you want to get one?

Q2: Do you think driving a car is relaxing? Or is it stressful? Explain.

Q3: Have you ever been in a car accident? What happened?

Q4: What do you think of AI (Artificial Intelligence)? Do we need it?

Q5: Do you think it's costly to own a car? Why? Why not?

Q6: Would you rather drive a car or be driven in a driverless car? Explain.

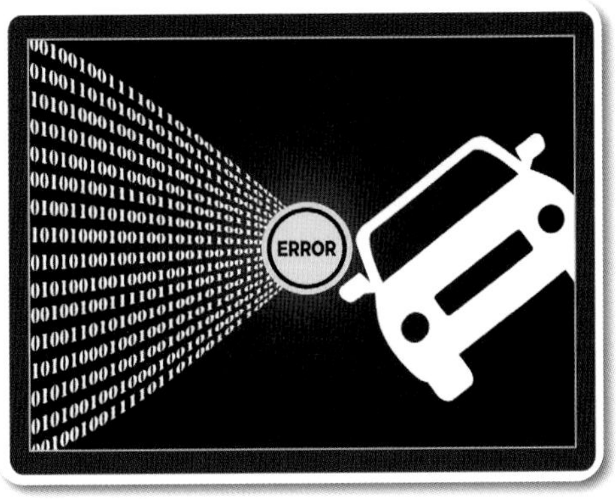

D Vocabulary

1 *Match the words on the left with the BEST meaning on the right.*

A) pricey means ____	1. dangerous; not safe
B) hazardous means ____	2. not dangerous
C) comfortable means ____	3. costly or expensive
D) creepy means ____	4. weird or scary; not a good feeling
E) safe means ____	5. you can save money; cheaper
F) economical means ____	6. nice and relaxing

2 *Read the list of words in the yellow box. Decide which words are probably Pros and which ones are Cons for the topic of* ***driverless cars****. Write P (Pro) or C (Con) in front of the word.*

C hazardous	____ economical	____ creepy
____ comfortable	____ safe	____ pricey

E Discussion Practice

1 *Read the dialogs below with a classmate. Decide on the answers together. Write your answers. Cover the dialogs and practice with your partner. Switch roles. Use your information from the dialogs to support your opinion.*

Q & A1

A: Why do you think a driverless car would be safe?

B: Umm, it would be safe because *it's a computer. It doesn't make mistakes. Also, it can react faster than a human driver. And,* ____________.

....

Q & A2

A: Why do you think a driverless car could be hazardous?

B: Umm, it could be hazardous ______________________________

______________________________.

....

Q & A 3

A: Why do you think a driverless car could be economical?

B: Umm, it could be economical because ______________________________

____.

Q & A 4

A: Why do you think a driverless car could be pricey?

B: Umm, it could be pricey ______________________________

____.

Q & A 5

A: Why do you think a driverless car could be comfortable?

B: Umm, it could be comfortable ______________________________

____.

Q & A 6

A: Why do you think a driverless car could be creepy for some people?

B: Umm, it could be creepy for some people because ______________________________

____.

2 *Using the information and/or language from the lesson, have a discussion about driverless cars with a partner. Give 2 or more reasons for your opinion.*

A

I'm For/Against driverless cars because ________________.
I also think ________________.
How about you?

B

Umm, I agree with you.
I think ________________
________________.
OR
Sorry, but I disagree. I think
________________. And, I also think ________________.

← Repeat **A**'s points or add your own.

Smartphone or Laptop?

A Introducing the Topic

Read the passage. Answer the question.

Q: Why are many people using smartphones and not computers these days?

A: It's because smartphones have become ______________________.

Do We Even Need Computers These Days? 14

Everyone has heard of a smartphone. I mean, they're everywhere. People use them on buses and trains, in coffee shops — everywhere. In fact, these days, it's quite common to see smartphones being used even in the classroom.

In the past, we used to do many tasks with a computer, but now that smartphones have become much more powerful, many tasks we used to do on a computer can now be done on a smartphone. In the classroom, students use their smartphone to do research in class, to do online quizzes and assignments, but also to watch educational videos and even have discussions with classmates. Some students do not even own a computer. They think a smartphone is all they need. Is this true? Do we even need computers anymore?

Main Discussion Question:

If you had a choice between using a laptop (notebook) computer and using a smartphone to do online assignments, which would you choose?

I would choose

- a smartphone to do online assignments.
- a laptop to do online assignments.

B Listening – Understanding Various Viewpoints

Listen and choose the answers you hear. More than one answer is possible. 15

1. Cassandra thinks having a laptop computer is a good idea because
   a) it has more power than a smartphone
   b) it's handy
   c) it has a bigger screen
   d) it's not so expensive

2. Ayako thinks using a smartphone to do online assignments is better than using a laptop because
   a) laptops are expensive
   b) it's small and compact
   c) you do not need Wi-Fi to do online assignments
   d) smartphones are cheap

3. Chuck thinks using a laptop computer to do online assignments is better than using a smartphone because
   a) it's easier to type on a laptop
   b) you can do more on a laptop
   c) the screen is bigger
   d) laptops are vital these days

C Q & A

Ask a classmate the questions below. HINT: Some language in Part B can help.

Q1: Do you own a laptop computer? Would you like to have one? Why or why not?

Q2: Which is easier to use for class assignments; a laptop or a smartphone?

Q3: Is a smartphone sometimes inconvenient for doing school work?

Q4: What problems have you had using your smartphone in class?

Q5: When is a laptop inconvenient for doing online assignments?

D Vocabulary

1 *Match the words on the left with the BEST meaning on the right.*

A) inefficient means ______	1. it's pricey; it costs more money
B) compact means ______	2. it's too large and takes up space
C) expensive means ______	3. not useful or helpful; not effective; cannot do some things
D) efficient means ______	4. useful; practical; helpful; can do more things
E) bulky means ______	5. small; does not take up much space
F) cheaper means ______	6. not as expensive; costs less

2 *Read the list of words in the yellow box. Decide which words are probably Pros and which ones are Cons for talking about* ***Laptops and Smartphones****. Write P (Pro) or C (Con) in front of the word.*

C inefficient	______ compact	______ expensive
______ efficient	______ bulky	______ cheaper

3 *Work with a partner. Fill in the missing words and then practice the dialog with your partner. Use* ***ALL*** *the words once!*

bulky ~~pretty fast~~ difficult compact
powerful takes up has use slow are

Dialog 1

A: I think a smartphone is too ______________ for doing online class assignments.

B: Hmm, I disagree. I think a smartphone is *pretty fast* for doing online classwork. I mean, most smartphones these days ______________ quite ______________. They're like mini-computers.

A: Hmm, but I think it's more ______________ to do online assignments on a smartphone. I mean, a smartphone ______________ a small screen and it's hard to type on.

B: Well, those are good points, but a smartphone is nice and ______________. So, you can carry it easily. A laptop, on the other hand, is ______________ and ______________ room in your backpack.

A: Hmm, that's true. But I still would rather ______________ a laptop for doing online assignments.

Dialog 2

Work with a partner. Fill in the missing words to make a natural dialog. Share your dialog with the class. After any corrections (if necessary) practice the dialog with your partner. Different answers are possible.

smartphone	laptop	bulky	inefficient
expensive	compact	powerful	efficient

A: Would you rather have a **laptop** or a **smartphone** to do online assignments?

B: Umm, I would choose a ____________ because I think a ____________ is not as ____________ as a ____________. How about you?

A: Umm, I think a ____________ is more ____________ than a ____________. So, I would choose a ____________.

E Discussion Practice

Work with a partner. Discuss whether you would rather do online assignments on a smartphone or on a laptop? Follow the cues (patterns) in the speech bubbles. ***You don't have to write your responses.***

I think I'd rather have a laptop / smartphone for doing my online assignments.

Really? Why?

Well, for one thing, ____________________________.

AGREE

I agree. I also think ____________________________.

DISAGREE

That's a good point but ____________________________.

Unit
8 Online Dating

A Introducing the Topic

Read the passage. Answer the question.

Q: How can online dating services save you time?

A: They can save you time because ______________________.

Would You Ever Try Online Dating? 16

Have you ever heard of online dating sites? Online dating sites are sites where people can search for a boyfriend or girlfriend. Online dating sites are becoming more and more popular these days and new ones sprout up (appear) almost daily. While some people do not like the idea of using online dating sites to find a boyfriend or girlfriend, there are many people who think online dating sites are good for several reasons.

First, not everyone has time to go on dates until they find the perfect guy or girl. Online dating services can save you time because you do not have to go on a date first. You can find an interesting person just by going online.

Secondly, online dating sites are efficient. I mean, they are a quick and easy way to find a companion. You just make a profile and then you can start looking for people who might be a good match for you.

Finally, using an online dating service could be fun. It almost feels like a game.

Main Discussion Question:

Would you ever try an online dating service?

- Yes, I would.
- No, I wouldn't.

B Listening – Understanding Various Viewpoints

Listen and choose the answers you hear. More than one answer is possible. 17

1. Cassandra thinks online dating services are
   a) interesting   b) useful for some people
   c) pretty safe   d) not safe

2. Ayako thinks using an online dating service
   a) is common these days
   b) is unnatural
   c) is a lazy way to find a companion
   d) is embarrassing

3. Chuck thinks using an online dating service
   a) is convenient   b) is economical
   c) is time-saving   d) is time-consuming

C Q & A

Ask and answer the questions below with a classmate or in a small group.

Q1: Have you ever visited an online dating site? Do you know any?

Q2: Are you curious about online dating? Have you thought about it?
(interested in)

Q3: Do you know anyone who has tried an online dating site? Were they successful? (i.e. Did they find a boyfriend or girlfriend?)

Q4: Do you think people are honest when they write their profiles?

Q5: Would you be embarrassed using an online dating service? Why? Why not?
Umm, I would be embarrassed because .... /
I wouldn't be embarrassed because ...

D Vocabulary

1 *Match the words on the left with the BEST meaning on the right.*

A) time-consuming means ____	1. it can save you money
B) exciting means ____	2. it's too much; there are too many choices; stressful
C) risky means ____	3. it takes much time
D) efficient means ____	4. useful; practical; helpful; you don't waste time
E) overwhelming means ____	5. very interesting and fun
F) cost-effective means ____	6. dangerous; not safe

2 *Read the list of words in the box. Decide which words are probably Pros and which ones are Cons for the topic of* ***Online Dating****. Write P (Pro) or C (Con) in front of the word.*

__C__ time-consuming	____ overwhelming	____ risky
____ efficient	____ exciting	____ cost-effective

3 *Work in a group of three. Fill in the missing words and then practice the dialog with your classmates. Use* ***ALL*** *the words once!*

natural stay home go out ~~efficient~~ overwhelming
choose exciting search find choices

A: I think online dating is great! I mean, it's so ____*efficient*____. You don't have to ________ at all. You can just ________ for someone you're interested in from your home.

B: I agree. You can just ________. And, I think it's efficient like you said because it's easy to ________ someone with the same interests. And, you have lots of ________. I think online dating would be ________. It's like a game.

C: But I think it could also be ________ because you might have too many choices online. It could be hard to decide who to ________. I mean, you have to look at many profiles. And personally, I don't want to find someone online. I'd rather go on a date in person. It's more ________.

E Discussion Practice

Part 1 Read the instructions below!

Step 1 – *Read the statements. (Circle) a response for "Me" (yourself). Do this first!*

Step 2 – *Ask your classmate: "What did you choose for number _____?" (1,2,3 etc.) (Circle) their responses.*

A: What did you choose for number 1? (2,3,4,5,6)
B: I chose "I agree". / "I disagree". / "I'm not sure."
A: Why did you choose "I agree"? / "I disagree"?
B: I chose "I agree" because .... / I chose "I disagree" because ....

NS = Not Sure

	Me			My Classmate		
1. Online dating is probably easier than finding someone face-to-face.	I agree	I disagree	NS	I agree	I disagree	NS
2. Face-to-face dating is always better than online dating.	I agree	I disagree	NS	I agree	I disagree	NS
3. Online dating is risky.	I agree	I disagree	NS	I agree	I disagree	NS
4. It's easier to find a person who matches you through online dating.	I agree	I disagree	NS	I agree	I disagree	NS
5. Online dating can save you money.	I agree	I disagree	NS	I agree	I disagree	NS
6. Online dating seems exciting and interesting.	I agree	I disagree	NS	I agree	I disagree	NS

Part 2

*Work in a group of **three**. Create a short discussion dialog about online dating. Decide A, B, C roles.*

A: I think using an online dating service is **okay**. I mean, ______________________
Reason
______________________________________.

B: I agree. ______________________________________.
Reason

C: Umm, I'm sorry but I disagree. ______________________
Reason
______________________________________.

Unit 9

Being Famous – Advantages & Disadvantages

A Introducing the Topic

Read the passage. Answer the question.

Q: According to the reading passage, what is the biggest drawback for being famous?

A: The biggest drawback is that you probably ______________________.

I Want to be Famous! 18

Have you ever wondered what it would be like to be famous? Do you think your life would be better if you were famous? Or would it be worse?

Many of us dream of being loved by millions of people or of being wealthy. I mean, famous people seem to have it all, right? But is being famous really all it's cracked up to be?
(really a good thing?)

It's true, when you're famous you enjoy many things ordinary people do not, but not all famous people have simple, easy lives. Imagine not being able to go shopping any time you want because people are always trying to take your picture. If you are famous, you probably won't have much privacy. This is the biggest drawback. And, of course, not all people will love you. There are people who may not like you because you are famous.

Main Discussion Question:

Would you like to be famous?

- Yes, I would.
- No, I wouldn't.

B Listening – Understanding Various Viewpoints

Listen and choose the answers you hear. More than one answer is possible. 19

1. Cassandra would like to be famous because
   a) famous people have less stress in their lives
   b) people love you
   c) you don't have to worry about money
   d) your life is interesting and exciting

2. Ayako thinks famous people
   a) can help society
   b) have to be careful in public
   c) have stressful lives
   d) always have to look good in public

3. Chuck thinks
   a) being famous would be bad if you were a shy person
   b) famous people are the same as everybody else
   c) famous people should do more to help the world
   d) some famous people don't have many problems

C Q & A

Ask and answer the questions below with a classmate or in a small group.

Q1: Would you like to be loved by millions of people? Explain.

Q2: Would you rather be a famous musician, actor, or athlete? Explain.

Q3: Do you admire any famous people? Why? Or, why not?

Q4: What would you do if you were wealthy (rich)?

Q5: Do you think famous people have easy lives? Why? Or, why not?

D Vocabulary

1 *Match the words on the left with a word that has a similar meaning.*

A)	2	no freedom or privacy	1. wealthy
B)	____	respected; loved	2. restrictive
C)	____	very tiring	3. dangerous
D)	____	rich	4. influential
E)	____	risky	5. exhausting
F)	____	powerful; important	6. admired

2 *Fill in the blanks with* ***a word in red****. Decide if the opinion is a pro (P) or a con (C).*

C A) If you are famous, your life would be *restrictive*. I mean, you would have no freedom.

____ B) If you are famous, you could be ____________. I mean, you have power and people listen to you.

____ C) If you are famous, you might be ____________. I mean, you have a lot of money.

____ D) Famous people are often ____________. I mean, many people might respect and love you.

____ E) Being famous could be ____________. I mean, you have to be careful in public.

____ F) Being famous would be ____________. I mean, it would be tiring.

3 *Fill in the blanks with a word from the box. Use each word* ***only once****.*

a. look your best	b. easily	c. adore	d. desire	e. society	f. everywhere

A) If you are famous you might be **wealthy**. I mean, you can buy whatever you ____________.

B) If you are famous you might be **admired**. I mean, many people might ____________ you and follow you on SNS.

C) Being famous could be **exhausting**. I mean, it's tiring because you always have to ____________.

D) Being famous could be **dangerous**. I mean, sometimes crazy fans follow you ____________ you go.

E) If you are famous you might be **influential**. I mean, you have power to help ____________.

F) Being famous could be **restrictive**. I mean, you can't go anywhere you want ____________.

E Discussion Practice

Discuss the Pros and Cons of being famous. Students A & B will give the pros and students C & D will give the cons. ***OPTION: This dialog can be done with two students instead of four. Write down your ideas (as a team) after your discussion.***

Students *A* + B – Pros

A: "I think it would be great to be famous because ...

A: ____

____.

B: And if you're famous ______________________________

____

____."

Students *C* + D – *Cons*

C: "Well, it might be nice to be famous, but it does have some drawbacks.

C: For one thing, ______________________________________

____.

D: Another drawback about being famous is that ______________

____

____."

Unit 10

Hybrid Classes – The Way of the Future?

A Introducing the Topic

Read the passage. Answer the question.

Q: What is another meaning for hybrid class?

A: Another meaning for hybrid class is ____________ ____________ class.

Hybrid Classes

20

Most students these days have heard about online learning. In fact, because of the pandemic, many students around the world have taken classes online.

If you are a college student, chances are you have experienced a hybrid class. A hybrid class, also called a blended learning class, combines classroom learning (face-to-face) and online learning. In other words, some classes are in-person at school while other classes are online.

Although many students enjoy taking classes face-to-face because they want to experience campus life, more and more students are happy to combine online classes with in-person classes, especially if they enjoy studying at their own pace. How about you?

Main Discussion Question:

Do you think all classes should be hybrid classes in the future?

- Yes.
- No.

B Listening – Understanding Various Viewpoints

Listen and choose the answers you hear. More than one answer is possible. 21

1. Cassandra thinks hybrid classes are the best type of classes because
   a) they give you flexibility
   b) you can work during the day
   c) students can improve their computer skills
   d) they make classes more interesting

2. Ayako thinks hybrid classes should be optional because
   a) some students do not have a computer
   b) some students want face-to-face interaction every class
   c) everyone learns in different ways
   d) some students are not good with technology

3. Chuck thinks only in-person classes are necessary because
   a) students should experience campus life
   b) students already spend too much time on computers
   c) many students cannot focus on their online classes
   d) some students cannot afford to buy good computers

C Q & A *Ask and answer the questions below with a classmate or in a small group.*

Q1: Have you taken a hybrid class? What was the subject?

Q2: If you have taken a hybrid class, did you think it was easy?

Q3: Would you like to work during the day and study at night online?

Q4: Is studying online stressful sometimes? When? In what situations?

Q5: Is it important for students to study at their own pace?

Q6: Why is face-to-face interaction in a classroom important for some students?

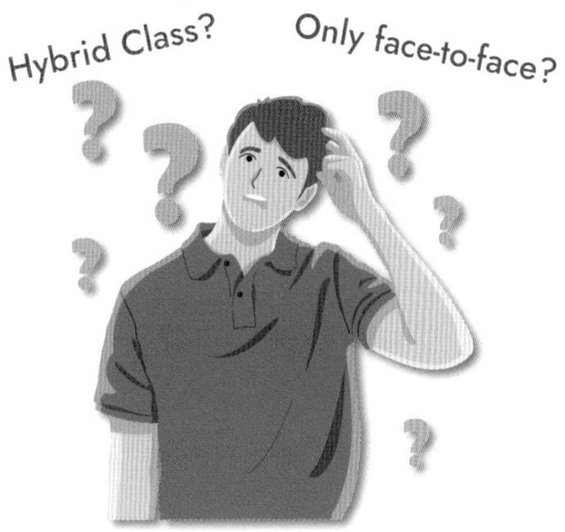

D Vocabulary

1 *Match the words on the left with the BEST meaning on the right.*

A) efficient means 5	1. difficult or hard; not easy
B) stimulating means _____	2. convenient; good for your schedule
C) frustrating means _____	3. not so useful; not productive
D) ineffective means _____	4. stressful; annoying
E) flexible means _____	5. helpful or useful: productive
F) demanding means _____	6. interesting; motivating; refreshing

2 *With a partner, fill in the blanks in the dialogs. Use the words in the box* **only once***. There are* **two** *extra words that do not fit the dialogs.*

frustrating	demanding	technology	during	organized	
creative	combining	efficient	pace	flexibility	while

Dialog 1

A: What's your opinion about hybrid classes? I mean, would you like all classes to be hybrid?

B: Umm, I'm not sure. I mean, I think you have to be very __________. Unfortunately, some people are not well-organized.

A: I agree. I also think some students are not good with __________. If they're not good with computers, an online class can be stressful or __________.

B: Good point. I do think, however, that __________ face-to-face learning and online learning is an __________ way to learn because you can meet your teacher and classmates weekly and you can also study at your own __________.

Dialog 2

A: What's your opinion about hybrid classes? I mean, would you like all classes to be hybrid?

B: Me? Yeah, I think it's a great idea! I mean, I have a part-time job so when I have a class online, I can work __________ the day and do the online stuff at night.

A: Yeah, me too. I really like the __________ of hybrid classes. I mean, you can take the classes whenever and wherever you want. They might be a bit challenging or __________ for some students, but I still think hybrid classes are the way to go.

E Discussion Practice

*With a partner, fill in the blanks in the dialogs. Use words from the box for RED blanks. Use your own language for parts that require an explanation (or example). Your dialogs must make sense. You can use the words in **black** if you need help or ideas.*

demanding efficient frustrating convenient
ineffective stimulating flexible boring
can work comfortable lose focus pace lazy
ask the teacher meet interaction/interact

Dialog 1

A: I think all the classes next year should be hybrid classes.

B: Really? Why do you think so?

A: Well, I think hybrid classes are good because they are ______________. I mean, ______________________________. (explain)

B: Umm, that's a good point. But I think hybrid classes can be ______________. ______________________________. (explain)

A: Hmm, I didn't think about that. You have a good point.

Dialog 2

A: What's your opinion about hybrid classes? You know, mixing face-to-face classes with online classes?

B: Umm, I don't want to do online classes.

A: Why not?

B: Well, I think online classes are ______________. I mean, ______________________________. (explain)

A: Umm, I like the idea of hybrid classes because they are ______________. I mean, ______________________________. (explain)

B: Hmm, ... that's a good point. I guess it depends on the person.

Compare your dialogs with another group's dialogs.

Unit 11

Working 4 Days a Week or 5 Days a Week?

A Introducing the Topic

Read the passage. Answer the question.

Q: What is a new idea some companies are thinking about?

A: Some employers are thinking about a ______________ workweek. In this case, the employees would work ______________ hours a day.

Work! Work! Work!

22

Most students will eventually (some day), have to work. Some may work part time, but many will work full time. In many countries around the world, it's common to work 5 days a week. It's also normal to work 8 hours a day. Of course, some people work overtime, but an 8-hour-a-day, 5-day workweek is the most common workweek. That however, may change in the future.

Some employers are toying with the idea (thinking about) of a four-day workweek. Employees would work 10-hour days instead of eight. While some people are excited about having a three-day weekend, others would rather work 8 hours a day instead of ten and have the normal, two-day weekend. They think working ten hours a day would leave them exhausted (very tired).

Main Discussion Question:

If you had a choice between working ten hours a day — four days a week and eight hours a day — five days a week, which workweek would you choose?

I would choose

- a four-day, 10-hour-a-day workweek with a three-day weekend.
- a five-day, 8-hour-a-day workweek with a two-day weekend.

B Listening – Understanding Various Viewpoints

Listen and choose the answers you hear. More than one answer is possible. 23

1. Chuck would work 10 hours a day, four days a week, but it would depend on
   a) the salary b) the type of job
   c) his boss d) if he was the boss

2. Cassandra would not work 10 hours a day, four days a week because
   a) it would be exhausting
   b) she is lazy
   c) she might become lazy
   d) she wants more free time

3. Ayako isn't sure about working 10 hours a day, four days a week because
   a) she has never done it b) 8 hours is common
   c) she is very busy d) she wants a normal job

C Q & A

Ask and answer the questions below with a partner or in a small group.

Q1: Do you think working 10 hours a day is unhealthy? Explain.

Q2: Do you think working 4 days a week, 10 hours a day will give you more energy? Explain.

Q3: Do you think a person who has a 3-day weekend will become lazy at work? Explain.

Q4: Are you happy just to work a 5-day, 8-hour-a-day job?

Q5: Do you think employees should have a choice about how many hours a week they work?

D Vocabulary

1 *Make your own statements using words from the box and your own ideas. Talk to a classmate and find out what they think. Circle and write their responses.*
Suggestion: Look back at the listening section (Part B) for some ideas for reasons.

okay	crazy	normal	better	interesting
a bit tiring	exhausting	type of job	salary	unhealthy

1. I think it's ________ to work 10 hours a day. What do you think?

   a) I agree. I think .... (+ reason)
   b) I disagree. I think .... (+ reason)
   c) I'm not sure.
   d) It depends on the ________.

2. I think it's better to work ________ hours a day, ________ days a week. What do you think?

   a) I agree. I think .... (+ reason)
   b) I disagree. I think .... (+ reason)
   c) I'm not sure.
   d) It depends on the ________.

3. I'd prefer to work full time, ________ days a week. How about you?

   a) Yeah, me, too. I think .... (+ reason)
   b) I think I'd prefer ________ days a week, because .... + reason
   c) It depends on the ________.

4. For me, it would be ________ to work more than 8 hours a day. How about for you?

   a) Umm, for me, it would be ________.
   b) Same here. (= Me, too. / I agree)

2 *Work with a partner and fill in the blanks with your own language. Then compare your dialog with another pair's dialog.*

A: I think if you work four days a week you'll have more time to ________
________.
You'll also have more time to ________.

B: Yeah, maybe, but if you work four days a week and longer days, you'll have less time ________.
And, you'll ________.

E Discussion Practice

Would you rather ...?

Would you rather work ten hours a day, four days a week or eight hours a day, five days a week? In pairs or groups of four, discuss giving PROS and CONS.

Students A & B go first and then Students C & D.

4-day week

PROS

Student A: I would rather work ten hours a day — four days a week because ...

Student B: I would rather work ten hours a day — four days a week because ...

5-day week

CONS

Student C: I would rather work eight hours a day — five days a week because ...

Student D: Me, too. I'd rather work eight hours a day — five days a week because ...

When you have finished your role plays, change groups and perform the dialogs again.

Example: The Pro team performs again with a different Con team.

Unit 12

Married at 35

A Introducing the Topic

Read the passage. Answer the question.

Q: According to the reading passage, what did Bruce have?

A: He had a ______________. In other words, he had saved quite a bit of money.

Getting Married Later in Life

24

Megan was thinking about her upcoming (near future) wedding. She had just turned 35 and was going to marry the man of her dreams. Still, she thought about how comfortable her life was. She had freedom to do whatever she wanted, and she had a great job. Best of all, she wasn't responsible for anybody else – only herself. Now that she was going to get married, she had another person to think about.

Bruce, was going to turn 37 in a few months. He wondered if he had waited too long to get married. Megan was a terrific woman, but he was a bit worried because he always wanted lots of kids. They were both in their 30's so he wasn't sure how many kids they could have. On the other hand, he had a nice nest egg (strong savings) and felt getting married was a good decision financially.

Main Discussion Question:

Would you like to get married at age 35?

- Yes, I would.
- No, I wouldn't.

B Listening – Understanding Various Viewpoints

Listen and choose the answers you hear. More than one answer is possible. 25

1. Cassandra thinks getting married later in life might be a challenge (might be difficult)
   a) for couples who want to have many children
   b) because it's harder to find a partner when you're older
   c) if you enjoy being single
   d) because older people don't like changes so much

2. Ayako thinks getting married at age 35 or older is
   a) becoming more common
   b) great for couples who do not want children
   c) better because couples are more mature
   d) harder when the kids get older

3. Chuck thinks
   a) older couples have more financial security
   b) when you get married later in life you have more life experiences
   c) it's okay to get married in your 20's if you are mature
   d) it's okay to get married in your 20's if you are responsible

C Q & A

Ask and answer the questions below with a classmate or in a small group.

Q1: Are there any benefits for getting married young? What are some?

Q2: At what age did your parents get married? Were they in their 20's?

Q3: Do you want to have children some day? If "Yes" how many kids do you want?

Q4: Do you think people who get married later in life have stronger marriages? Why? Why not?
(better relationships than younger couples)

Q5: Should you get married if you do not have much money? Why? Why not?

D Vocabulary

1 *Match the words on the left with a word that has a similar meaning.*

A) ______	more adult; more experienced	1. economical
B) ______	extremely tiring	2. stubborn
C) ______	time to do what you want	3. risky
D) ______	cost-effective; have more money	4. mature
E) ______	unsafe; dangerous	5. exhausting
F) ______	inflexible; not easy to change	6. freedom

2 *Fill in the blanks with* ***a word in red****. Decide if the opinion is a pro (P) or a con (C).*

C A) Having a baby at the age of 35 is sometimes a bit risky for some women.

______ B) If you get married later in life, you have more ______ to do what you like.

______ C) People in their 30's can be ______. I mean, they don't change their ways easily.

______ D) Getting married later in life could be ______. I mean, you can save more money for your future.

______ E) Taking care of many children if you are older could be ______.

______ F) Couples in their 30's are generally more ______ and responsible.

3 *Fill in the blanks with a word from the box.*

a. put off	b. boring	c. responsible	d. view	e. stubborn	f. anytime

A) I think it's okay to ______ getting married until your 30's. You don't have to hurry.

B) I think when you get older, you are a bit more ______. I mean, you like to do things your own way.

C) I think men can get married ______. I mean, it's easier for them.

D) I think marriage in your 30's could be a bit ______. I mean, life is more exciting in your 20's.

E) Older people are generally more ______. I mean, they are more reliable and mature.

F) I think when you are older, you have a better ______ of life.

E Discussion Practice

Discuss the Pros and Cons of getting married at age 35. Students A & B will give the pros and students C & D will give the cons. **OPTION: This dialog can be done with two students instead of four. Write down your ideas (as a team) after your discussion.**

Students A + B - Pros

A: "I think getting married at age 35 is perfectly fine for a ***woman/man/couple*** *because*

A: ______________________________

______________________________.

B: I agree. I also think getting married at 35 or older is better for a **woman/man/couple** because

____

______________________________."

Students C + D - Cons

C: "Those are good points. However, getting married later in life also has drawbacks.

C: For one thing, ______________________________

______________________________.

D: Another drawback about getting married at age 35 is that ______________________________

____

______________________________."

When you have finished your role plays, change groups and perform the dialogs again.

Example: The Pro team performs again with a different Con team.

Unit
13 Cosmetic Surgery

A Introducing the Topic

Read the passage. Answer the question.

Q: What is liposuction?

A: Liposuction is a medical procedure where ______________ is ______________ from the body.

Cosmetic Surgery 26

You may have heard the term cosmetic surgery from a friend or from the Internet, or on TV. Cosmetic surgery is a procedure at a hospital where a part of the body is changed. It is different from plastic surgery which is surgery to repair your body.

Sometimes we think only movie stars have cosmetic surgery but millions of "everyday folks" (regular people) have cosmetic surgery, too.

Cosmetic surgery can be done on the face or the body. One of the most popular medical procedures is liposuction, where fat is removed from a part of the body such as the thighs or stomach. Other popular cosmetic surgeries are for changing the shape of the nose and eyes, or to remove wrinkles on the face.

Many people may think cosmetic surgery is most often done on older people, but these days, younger people are getting it, too. Even young women and men in their 20's are getting cosmetic surgery.

Main Discussion Question:

Do you think it's okay for people in their 20's to get cosmetic surgery?

- Yes.
- No.

remove wrinkles
change my eyelids
get a hair transplant
change the shape of my _____
get a tummy tuck
fuller lips
smaller ____________________

BEFORE FACE INJECTION SURGERY AFTER

B Listening – Understanding Various Viewpoints

Listen and choose the answers you hear. More than one answer is possible. 27

1. Cassandra thinks getting cosmetic surgery
   a) is a person's choice
   b) seems painful
   c) is something older people get
   d) isn't necessary because appearance is not the most important thing about a person

2. Ayako thinks getting cosmetic surgery is
   a) sometimes risky
   b) not necessary for most people
   c) becoming more popular with young people
   d) good for improving a person's confidence

3. Chuck would get cosmetic surgery if
   a) he was older
   b) he was not confident about his appearance
   c) it was safe
   d) he had lots of money

C Q & A *Work with a partner or small group and write answers to the questions.*

Q1: Why do you think most people get cosmetic surgery?

A1: I think they do it ______________________________

____

____

Q2: If you could change one thing about your appearance, would you change anything? If "Yes", what would you change? Give a reason. If "No", why not?

A2: I would change ______________________________. (Classmate 1)

A2: I would change ______________________________. (Classmate 2)

Q3: Your best friend just had a nose job. You didn't know and you meet her. What do you say?

1. Wow! You look ______________________________!

2. Oh, my gosh! Why ______________________________?

3. Umm, ... you look .... different.

4. (other) ______________________________

D Vocabulary

1 *Match the words on the left with the BEST meaning on the right.*

A) surgery means ____	1. dangerous or unsafe
B) appearance means ____	2. negative points of our body
C) irreversible means ____	3. have enough money to pay for something
D) imperfections means ____	4. you cannot change it after you do it
E) risky means ____	5. an operation or procedure at a hospital
F) afford means ____	6. what you look like

2 *Use words from Part D (Red words) to complete the sentences. Use words* ***ONLY once****!*

1. I think some people want to hide their ____________. They want to be perfect.
2. Cosmetic surgery is often ____________. You cannot undo it.
3. I'd have cosmetic surgery but I don't think I could ____________ it.
4. Many people want to change something about their ____________.
5. My friend had ____________ recently because she wanted a flatter tummy.
6. It's always ____________ when you have surgery.

3 *Choose a word to complete the statements. Choose* ***T*** *(True)* ***F*** *(False) or* ***NS*** *(Not sure). Discuss your answers with a partner or in a small group.*

right happy negative unhappy chance

1. People should be ____________ with how they look. T / F / NS
2. People have a ____________ opinion of people who have had cosmetic surgery. T / F / NS
3. Everyone has the ____________ to change their appearance. T / F / NS
4. You might be ____________ even after you have cosmetic surgery. T / F / NS

E Discussion Practice

*With a partner, fill in the blanks in the dialogs. Use words from the box for the RED blanks in dialog 1. Use your own language for parts that require an explanation (or example). Your dialogs must make sense. You can use the words in **black** if you need help or ideas.*

eyelids eyebrows lips nose tummy
cheeks chin thighs butt
look better appearance hide imperfections
afford risky irreversible surgery

Dialog 1

A: I'm thinking about getting cosmetic surgery on my ____________________.

B: Really? Why do you want to get cosmetic surgery on your ____________________?

A: Umm, because I ____.

B: **(Give a response)** ____

____.

Dialog 2

A: What's your opinion about cosmetic surgery? I mean, do you think people have better lives after they get cosmetic surgery?

B: Hmm, I don't know.

A: But what do you think?

B: Well, I ____

____

____.

What do you think?

A: Me? Umm, I think ____

____.

Unit 14

Goodbye SNS!

A Introducing the Topic

Read the passage. Find the word in the passage that fits the blank.

Q: What does ______________ mean?

A: It means you cannot stop doing something easily.

SNS – Do We Need Them?

28

Practically everyone with access to the Internet knows about social networking services or SNS for short. SNS basically means social media. Popular SNS include Twitter, Facebook, Instagram and now TikTok.

SNS are popular because they can connect users easily, and because the content on SNS is often interesting. For example, you can learn about your favorite celebrity's life or you can send your friend a photo of a great dish you had at a restaurant on SNS. It's even a good way to meet people from other countries.

Although there are definitely benefits for using SNS, there are also drawbacks. For example, they can be addictive. Many users feel they have to check their SNS hundreds of times a day. They just cannot stop checking their SNS. Another drawback is the amount of time users spend on their SNS. Research shows many users spend at least five hours a day on SNS. That's a lot of time.

Main Discussion Question:

Do you think you could live without SNS?

- Yes, I could live without SNS.
- No, I could not live without SNS.

B Listening – Understanding Various Viewpoints

Listen and choose the answers you hear. More than one answer is possible. 29

1. Cassandra says she quit using social media because
   a) it was stressful
   b) there is too much information
   c) she prefers to use email
   d) her grades have gone down this year

2. Ayako says using social media
   a) can be stressful
   b) can be exhausting
   c) is a great way to meet new people
   d) is valuable for people who work

3. Chuck thinks SNS
   a) is useful for communicating with the world
   b) is useful but not vital.
   c) is a great way to relieve stress
   d) can be overwhelming and stressful at times

C Q & A

Ask and answer the questions below with a classmate or in a small group.

Q1: Do you use SNS? What sort of (= kind of) SNS do you use?

Q2: Do you think SNS can help with job hunting? How?

Q3: Using SNS can be too much and make you feel tired or stressed out. Why?

Q4: How many hours a day do you visit social media sites?

Q5: Do you think SNS can be good for your mental health? How?

Q6: Why do you think some famous people quit using social media?

D Vocabulary

1 *Match the words on the left with the BEST meaning on the right.*

A) valuable means ______	1. fun; fun to do; enjoyable
B) entertaining means ______	2. it takes up a lot of your time
C) overwhelming means ______	3. there are benefits or good things you can get
D) addictive means ______	4. you feel refreshed
E) time-consuming means ______	5. controlling; it's difficult to stop doing it
F) relaxing means ______	6. sometimes it is too much; stressful; exhausting

2 *With a partner, fill in the blanks in the dialogs. Use the words in the box* **only once**. *There are 2 extra words!*

communication quit keep in touch tiring time-consuming
controlling overwhelming cancelling tired relaxing

Dialog 1

A: I haven't seen you on Twitter or Instagram recently. Everything OK?

B: Umm, actually, I ______________ using SNS.

A: You're kidding. Why?

B: Umm, it was ______________ my life. I mean, it's so ______________. Every day I was spending more than five hours checking all my accounts. And I hate posting responses sometimes. It's ______________. I mean, it's just too much!

Dialog 2

A: I'm thinking about ______________ all my SNS accounts.

B: Really? Why?

A: Umm, I'm just ______________ of listening to negative news and negative comments.

B: But how will you ______________ with everybody?

A: Umm, I'll just phone them or email them.

B: Well, I know sometimes social media takes up much of your time, but it's also fun and ______________.

E Discussion Practice

Discuss the Pros and Cons of using social media. Students A & B will give the pros and students C & D will give the cons. **OPTION: This dialog can be done with two students instead of four. Write down your ideas (as a team) after your discussion.**

Students A + B - Pros

A: "I think social media is necessary because ...

A: ____

____.

B: And I think we need social media sites because ______________________

____

____."

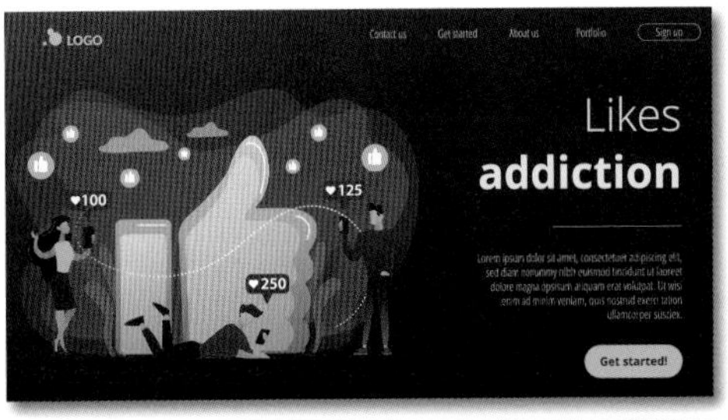

Students C + D - Cons

C: "Umm, it's true, social media has benefits, but there are also drawbacks.

C: For one thing, ____

____.

D: Another drawback is ____

____

____."

When you have finished your role plays, change groups and perform the dialogs again.

Example: The Pro team performs again with a different Con team.

Unit 15

Working From Home – Advantages & Disadvantages

A Introducing the Topic

Read the passage. Answer the question.

Q: How many drawbacks can you find in the reading passage?

A: I could find ______________ drawbacks in the reading passage.

Working From Home

30

What do you think about having a job where you work at home instead of an office? Would you like this work environment? Or, would you prefer to work at an office with other people? Working at home sounds like the perfect job, but it's not for everybody.

Working from home gives you more freedom, but for some people, too much freedom means it's harder to get things done. For instance, you might think you can do your work a bit later in the day and then discover that you didn't get anything done.

Another drawback is the lack of social interaction. I mean, if you only work at home, you don't talk to other people face-to-face. Social skills are important in daily life.

Finally, working from home might be too comfortable. Your sofa or bed is close by and that 15-minute nap you want to take, might become a 2 or 3-hour nap.

Main Discussion Question:

If you had a choice between working at home or working at an office, which would you choose?

- working at home
- working at an office

B Listening – Understanding Various Viewpoints

Listen and choose the answers you hear. More than one answer is possible. 31

1. Cassandra thinks working at home
   a) could be distracting
   b) is not stressful because no one is watching you
   c) is too comfortable
   d) is not comfortable

2. Ayako believes working at home
   a) could be relaxing
   b) would be exhausting
   c) is good because you can do better work
   d) is less stressful than working at an office

3. Chuck thinks
   a) the work environment is not so important
   b) the work environment is more comfortable at home
   c) working in an office is sometimes stressful
   d) working in an office is comfortable but stressful

C Q & A

Ask and answer the questions below with a classmate or in a small group.

Q1: Do you think working face-to-face with co-workers is important? Explain.

Q2: Do you think people who work from home are better at their jobs? Explain.

Q3: Do you think working from home is good for shy people? Explain.

Q4: Do you think most people will be distracted working from home? Why? Why not?

Q5: Do you think young people are responsible enough to work from home? Explain.

D Vocabulary

1 *Go through the vocabulary (a – h). Look up any words you don't know. Discuss the question below with a classmate or in a small group. List your answers on the line below.*

What sort of person would be suitable working from home?

A: *I think that if you work from home, you must be ______________________.*

B: *Umm, I agree with all your choices. OR B: Umm, I agree with all your choices except I think you don't have to be ______________________ to work from home.*

a) a responsible person
b) a hard-working person
c) a creative person
d) an independent person
e) a highly intelligent person
f) a person who works well by themselves
g) a very energetic person
h) an irresponsible person

Go back through A's answers. Try to give reasons for your answers. Example: ... must be a creative person because you might have to think of your own ideas sometimes. Report your choices to another group. Compare answers.

2 *Go through the vocabulary (a – h). Look up any words you don't know. Discuss the question below with a classmate or in a small group. List your answers on the line below.*

What sort of person would not be suitable working from home?

A: *I think that if you are ______________________, you should not work from home.*

B: *Umm, I agree with all your choices. OR B: Umm, I agree with all your choices except I think if you are ______________________, you can still work from home.*

a) an irresponsible person
b) easily distracted
c) not independent
d) a person who depends on others
e) a shy person
f) a person who likes working face-to-face
g) a very energetic person
h) a lazy person

Go back through A's answers. Try to give reasons for your answers. Example: ... easily distracted you should not work from home because you will watch TV or check your SNS instead of working. Report your choices to another group. Compare answers.

E Discussion Practice

■ *Discuss the Pros and Cons of working from home. Student A will give the pros and student B will give the cons.*

Student A — Ask Q1 and Q2 and then give two reasons for your final opinion.
Student B — Give answers for A1 and A2.

Look at Page 64 for vocabulary!

A(Q1): What kind of person are you? Please describe yourself.

B(A1): Umm, I'm ______________, ______________ and ______________.

A(Q2): And, are you ______________? (creative / an independent person, etc.)

B(A2): Umm, yeah, I think so. / Umm, no, I'm not. / Umm, maybe. I'm not sure.

A: Opinion: In my opinion, working from home might be suitable for you / might not be suitable for you because ______________.

■ *Make your own statements using words from the box and your own ideas. Talk to a classmate and find out what they think. Circle and write their responses.*

okay	more relaxing	boring	better
a bit tiring	person	type of job	distracting

1. I think working from home might be ______________.
   a) I agree. + reason b) I disagree. + reason c) I'm not sure. d) It depends on the ______________.
2. I think it's ______________ to work with other people face-to-face than at home.
   a) I agree. + reason b) I disagree. + reason c) I'm not sure. d) It depends on the ______________.
3. Only people who are very responsible can work from home.
   a) I agree. + reason b) I disagree. + reason c) I'm not sure. d) It depends on the ______________.
4. Working from home could be ______________ because you can do other things easily.
   a) I agree. + reason b) I disagree. + reason c) I'm not sure. d) It depends on the ______________.

著作権法上、無断複写・複製は禁じられています。

What Do You Think? [B-948]
15 Topics for Discussion & Conversation
15のトピックから学ぶ英語ディスカッション

1刷 2023年3月15日

著　者 Alan Bossaer

発行者 南雲　一範　Kazunori Nagumo
発行所 株式会社　南雲堂
〒162-0801　東京都新宿区山吹町361
NAN'UN-DO Co., Ltd.
361 Yamabuki-cho, Shinjuku-ku, Tokyo 162-0801, Japan
振替口座 : 00160-0-46863
TEL: 03-3268-2311（営業部:学校関係）
03-3268-2384（営業部:書店関係）
03-3268-2387（編集部）
FAX: 03-3269-2486

編集者 加藤　敦

組　版 柴崎　利恵

装　丁 銀月堂

検　印 省　略

コード ISBN978-4-523-17948-1 C0082

Printed in Japan

E-mail : nanundo@post.email.ne.jp
URL : https://www.nanun-do.co.jp/